RUNES OF DRAGONS

www.runesofdragons.com

by EnglishMystic

EnglishMystic

Copyright © 2024 Kevin Paul Humphrey
All rights reserved.

ISBN: 9798879173048
Imprint: Independently published

An Introduction

Kevin Paul Humphrey {EnglishMystic}

Hello Dear Reader, I'm Kev.

I use the name EnglishMystic, because I live in England, and I love all things Mystical.

From an early age, I saw Lions in my bedroom, horse heads on the pillow, and shoes walking across the landing!

And as I've gone through life I've experienced a lot of mystical events, from Dragons visiting me in the English countryside, while I hacked out, on the horse I am the human too, through visitations from wise ancestors, deep realisations during a Vipassana 10-day monk-like retreat, to connections with Pachamama in Peru while visiting Machu Picchu and numerous other learnings during my Remembering, through studying Reiki (Master), Rahanni Celestial energy healer and Shamanism (Diploma in Healing) & during my time as a Life Coach with SatoriPrime. And more recently twenty-seven Dragons requesting I introduce them to the world with their Runes and Artwork.

More than a decade ago I started to remember my Magick, a decade before that I had my first true Dark Night of The Soul, as my Soul stirred me from my slumber, so I know what it's like to start to remember and how confusing it can be.

I moved from an almost four-decade career in computer software into mystical teachings and healings. With a fair amount of overlap in time, as I transitioned to full-time EnglishMystic.

My role, mission, my Dharma, is to provide you with a memory jog so that you can remember for yourself how Magical you are and help you tap into your Higher Purpose for this lifetime.

If you have any questions, please let me know and I'll be happy to assist.

I hope you enjoy this book, as much as I did, listening to the Dragons as they shared their Wisdom, Runes, and Artworks.

Much Love

Kev, the EnglishMystic

Biography & Links

I am a seasoned Entrepreneur, and Information Technology expert with nearly four decades in the field, now a Master in the Mystical Realms. Based near the enchanting Dartmoor National Park in Devon, England, I've delved deep into the world of Energy Healing within Shamanism, becoming a Reiki Master, Rahanni Celestial Energy Healer, and a dedicated practitioner of ancient Shamanic arts.

It doesn't stop there, my connection with Dragons is a central part of the journey. I'm not only a Dragon Shaman but also a passionate teacher, spreading the wisdom of Shamanism and guiding people on how to connect with their very own spirit team, particularly their Dragon guides.

Meet Your Dragon Guides:
https://www.meetyourdragons.com/
Web: https://www.englishmystic.com/
Facebook: https://www.facebook.com/EnglishMystic
Instagram: https://www.instagram.com/englishmystic/
YouTube:
https://www.youtube.com/@KevinHumphreyVideo
TikTok: https://www.tiktok.com/@englishmystic
Linkedin: https://www.linkedin.com/in/englishmystic/

Books by Kevin Humphrey / EnglishMystic

MERLIN, THE MYSTICAL BARD, Transmissions, Spells & Chants

Galactic Mysticism: EnglishMystic's, Ritual and Ceremony for Healing and Wisdom

Fly With Dragons

Table of Contents

AN INTRODUCTION **3**
    BIOGRAPHY & LINKS 5
    RUNES BLESSING 10
    WELCOME TO THE RUNES OF DRAGONS 11

THE DRAGON RUNES **12**

WHERE ARE THE RUNES FROM? **13**

HOW TO USE THE RUNES & ARTWORK **14**
    *BREATHING CONSCIOUSLY 15
    BOX BREATHING EXERCISE 15

DRAGON BREATHING EXERCISE **17**

BLESSINGS OF THE DRAGON RUNES **19**

DRAGON RUNES ALTAR **20**

HALL OF DRAGON RUNES CEREMONY **23**

#1 THE MEANING OF THE RAINBOW DRAGON **29**
    THE RAINBOW DRAGON RUNE: 30
    THE RAINBOW DRAGON ART: 30

#2 THE MEANING OF THE CHAKRA DRAGON **31**

#3 THE MEANING OF THE WATER DRAGON **35**
    THE WATER DRAGON RUNE: 36
    THE WATER DRAGON ART: 36

#4 THE MEANING OF THE AIR DRAGON **37**
    THE AIR DRAGON RUNE: 38
    THE AIR DRAGON ART: 38

#5 THE MEANING OF THE FIRE DRAGON **39**
    THE FIRE DRAGON RUNE: 40
    THE FIRE DRAGON ART: 40

#6 THE MEANING OF THE EARTH DRAGON 41
The Earth Dragon Rune: 42
The Earth Dragon Art: 42

#7 THE MEANING OF THE SPIRIT DRAGON 43
The Spirit Dragon Rune: 44
The Spirit Dragon Art: 44

#8 THE MEANING OF THE NORTH DRAGON 45
The North Dragon Rune: 46

#9 THE MEANING OF THE EAST DRAGON 47
The East Dragon Rune: 48
The East Dragon Art: 48

#10 THE MEANING OF THE SOUTH DRAGON 49
The South Dragon Rune: 50
The South Dragon ART: 50

#11 THE MEANING OF THE WEST DRAGON 51
The West Dragon Rune: 52
The West Dragon Art: 52

#12 THE MEANING OF THE MIND DRAGON 53
The Mind Dragon Rune: 54
The Mind Dragon Art: 54

#13 THE MEANING OF THE SOUL DRAGON 55

#14 THE MEANING OF THE BODY DRAGON 57
The Body Dragon Rune: 58

#15 THE MEANING OF THE AURA DRAGON 59
The Aura Dragon Rune: 60
The Aura Dragon Art: 60
The Iron Dragon Rune: 62

#17 THE MEANING OF THE WOOD DRAGON 63
The Wood Dragon Rune: 64

#18 THE MEANING OF THE STONE DRAGON 65
- THE STONE DRAGON RUNE: 66
- THE STONE DRAGON ART: 66

#19 THE MEANING OF THE CRYSTAL DRAGON 69
- THE CRYSTAL DRAGON RUNE: 70

#20 THE MEANING OF THE ICE DRAGON 71
- THE ICE DRAGON RUNE: 72

#21 THE MEANING OF THE LAVA DRAGON 75
- THE LAVA DRAGON RUNE: 76
- THE LAVA DRAGON ART: 76

#22 THE MEANING OF THE GOLD DRAGON 79
- THE GOLD DRAGON RUNE: 80
- THE GOLD DRAGON ART: 80

#23 THE MEANING OF THE SILVER DRAGON 83
- THE SILVER DRAGON RUNE: 84
- THE SILVER DRAGON ART: 84
- THE COPPER DRAGON RUNE: 88
- THE COPPER DRAGON ART: 88

#25 THE MEANING OF THE DIAMOND DRAGON 91
- THE DIAMOND DRAGON ART: 92
- THE DIAMOND DRAGON ART: 92

#26 THE MEANING OF THE METEORITE DRAGON 95
- THE METEORITE DRAGON RUNE: 96
- THE METEORITE DRAGON ART: 96

#27 THE MEANING OF THE BLANK DRAGON 99
- THE BLANK RUNE: 100
- THE BLANK RUNE ART: 100

ENGLISHMYSTIC 103

LINKS 106

EnglishMystic

Runes Blessing

Blessings upon this sacred tome, a gateway to the realms where Dragon's roam. In the mystical pages, may the twenty-seven Dragons of the Runes awaken, their ancient wisdom and power unshaken.

Oh, mighty Dragons of the ancient script, guardians of knowledge and secrets cryptic. As Merlin once weaved his magic so fine, may these runes in your guidance intertwine.

May each symbol, a Dragon in disguise, bring forth ancient magic that never dies. With every turn of the page, let the reader find, the essence of the runes, in heart and mind.

In the spirit of Merlin's wise decree, let these Dragons guide, set the seeker free. Bless those who delve into this mystic art, may their journey be blessed, right from the start.

As the pages unfold, and the runes are cast, may the Dragons energy forever last. So, mote it be, in the realms of old, as the twenty-seven Dragons their tales unfold.

Blessings to you, dear Reader, as you embark on this magical quest, may your teachings soar and bring healing zest.

May the Dragons dance in your presence bright, as you share their wisdom, both day and night.

Welcome to the Runes of Dragons

You will learn about the twenty-seven Dragon runes, their meaning, and how combining them can create powerful Dragon magic.

As you learn about each of the runes, you will gain insight into the different aspects and elements of Dragons, such as light, energy, life, wind, fire, earth, spirit, and more.

We will explore how these Runes can be used to bring good luck, protection, guidance, and knowledge to the user.

Get ready to unlock the power of the twenty-seven Dragon Runes.

If you have not purchased the physical runes set, you can do so at www.RuneofDragons.com, though you do not need the physical runes to meet the Dragons of the Runes. The physical Runes are there to assist you as a tarot card would.

You will also see individual journeys to each Dragon of the Runes on that web page, you can purchase individual Dragons of the Runes, or purchase the twenty-seven set of drum-led shamanic journeys to the Dragons Grove.

The Dragon Runes

1. Rainbow Dragon - Light
2. Chakra Dragon - Energy
3. Water Dragon - Life
4. Air Dragon - Wind
5. Fire Dragon - Fire
6. Earth Dragon - Earth
7. Spirit Dragon - Spirit
8. North Dragon - North
9. East Dragon - East
10. South Dragon - South
11. West Dragon - West
12. Mind Dragon - Mind
13. Soul Dragon - Soul
14. Body Dragon - Body
15. Aura Dragon - Aura
16. Iron Dragon - Iron
17. Wood Dragon - Wood
18. Stone Dragon - Stone
19. Crystal Dragon - Crystal
20. Ice Dragon - Ice
21. Lava Dragon - Lava
22. Gold Dragon - Gold
23. Silver Dragon - Silver
24. Copper Dragon - Copper
25. Diamond Dragon - Diamond
26. Meteorite Dragon - Meteor
27. BLANK - Infinite

Where are the Runes from?

As a Dragon Rider, I have been gifted with twenty-seven Dragon Runes that represent the ancient wisdom and magic of the Dragons. These runes were not created using traditional methods and were instead produced through a combination of telepathic communication with the Dragons and advanced technology.

Through their powerful minds, the Dragons shared their knowledge and secrets with me, and together we crafted these intricate and beautiful runes and artworks. Each symbol holds a unique meaning and can unlock powerful abilities hidden within us all. The symbols are simple and easy to understand, both to the eye and the mind, and the Dragons are always reminding me that simplicity is the key, they say we humans Love to overthink and overcomplicate things.

The artwork for each Dragon is paired to the rune symbol and is more complicated to the eye and mind, however, it speaks from the Dragons hearts to ours and into our souls and need not be thought about too deeply, investigate the depths of the image and let your mind and thoughts relax, let your eyes lose focus and absorb the imagery into your third eye, into your very being and soul and know.

They say to connect with your Heart-Mind more than the mind of the head. It is suggested that you meet with each of the Dragons of the runes in turn and create a strong connection with them, as the truest wisdom comes from them, and the Runes are purely a simple method of connecting with them and the ultimate wisdom.

How to use the Runes & Artwork

The Dragons have gifted us with twenty-seven powerful Runes, each one imbued with their innate magic and wisdom.

These runes and their accompanying artworks were communicated to me both telepathically and through advanced technologies. To use these runes, one must focus their intention on a particular aspect of their life.

Sit in an open-hearted and meditative state, often *breathing consciously for a few minutes will help you get into a calm and open state of being, once you are sitting with a calm mind and a relaxed body, select a rune or pull one from the deck randomly, and consult the accompanying rune and artwork, and read the guidance.

Feel into the guidance, look for an extended time at the rune and artwork, let your eyes lose the sharp focus and pull the images into your heart, and feel into what resonates for you at this moment, leave the rest behind, and feel into your heart what is the message in this now.

The runes can provide insight, clarity, and assistance as we navigate the complexities of the world around us.

Allow the Dragon's magic to guide you on your journey.

Do use the exercises offered, they will help you connect with your Dragons to understand their messages better, as the ones I offer are my perspective and may well be off the mark, it is always best to ask the Dragons directly.

Tip:

The runes and artwork are a way in which your Dragons can communicate with you, by planting a seed of thought with you, to fully explore the reason for the message, the best way is to talk to the Dragon of the Rune.

You can do that through meditation or my preferred method is, a drum-led Shamanic journey to them, be that in the upper, or lower realms of reality.

I include a drum-led journey for you to open the portal to the lower realm, you can use this with the intention, as the intention is key, of meeting your Dragons - you can say

"I travel to the lower realms on this Shamanic journey to meet the Dragons of FIRE" and change fire to which ever Dragon you wish to connect with.

Breathwork for connecting to your Dragons

To get into a relaxed state before connecting with your Dragons, I suggest a breathing exercise, see below:

*Breathing Consciously
There are many breathwork exercises, here are two you could do, to get into the zone before meeting your Rune Dragon.

Box breathing exercise
The box breathing exercise is a breathing technique used to promote relaxation and reduce stress.

It is called box breathing because the pattern of breath is done in four equal counts, creating a box-like shape. Here's how you can do the box breathing exercise:

1. Find a quiet and comfortable place to sit or lie down.
2. Close your eyes and take a moment to relax your body and clear your mind.
3. Start by inhaling slowly through your nose to the count of four. Feel your abdomen rise as you fill your lungs with air.
4. Hold your breath for a count of four, feeling the fullness of your breath in your body.
5. Exhale slowly through your mouth to the count of four, feeling the release of tension as you let go of the air.
6. Pause for a count of four before starting the next breath cycle.
7. Repeat this pattern for a few minutes, focusing on the rhythm of your breath and the feeling of relaxation it brings.
8. If your mind wanders, gently bring your attention back to your breath and continue the pattern.

The box breathing exercise can be done anywhere and at any time to help you calm your mind and body, reduce anxiety, and increase overall well-being and connecting you to the Dragon energy of both Fire and Air at the same time and very useful to connect to any Rune Dragon.

Dragon breathing exercise

Another great one is the Dragon breathing exercise, it's a visualisation technique that can help release tension and promote a sense of empowerment.

It involves imagining yourself as a powerful dragon, breathing out fire to let go of negativity and stress.

Here's how you can practice the dragon breathing exercise:

1. Find a comfortable position where you can sit or stand with your spine straight.
2. Close your eyes and take a few deep breaths to relax your body and quiet your mind.
3. Visualise yourself as a majestic dragon, with scales, wings, and fiery eyes. Feel the power and strength of the dragon within you.
4. Take a deep breath in through your nose, drawing in positive energy and power. Imagine this energy filling your belly and chest as you inhale.
5. As you exhale through your mouth, imagine releasing a powerful stream of fire from your core. And release your shyness and roar like a Dragon expelling fire through its mouth and nostrils. Visualise the fire burning away any stress, negativity, or tension that you are holding onto.
6. Continue this pattern of deep inhales through the nose, and forceful roaring exhales through the mouth, imagining yourself breathing out fire with each exhale.
7. As you breathe out, let go of any negative emotions or thoughts that no longer serve you. Feel a sense of release and empowerment with each breath.

8. Repeat this dragon breathing exercise for at least 10 exhales or until you feel a sense of calm and renewed energy.

By channelling your inner dragon and visualising the release of fire, this exercise can help you feel more empowered and in control, while also promoting relaxation and stress relief and connecting you to Dragon energy of both Fire and Air at the same time and very useful to connect to any Rune Dragon.

Blessings of the Dragon Runes

Each Dragon of the Runes has its own blessing for you, I list them here in alphabetical order and list the rune number # too.

Rune	#	BLESSING
Air Dragon - Wind	4	"Bridging realms, where magic overwhelms."
Aura Dragon - Aura	15	"Dragon's breath, life's mysteries unearth."
BLANK - Infinite	27	"From heart to hand, blessings expand."
Body Dragon - Body	14	"Awaken strength, in every length."
Chakra Dragon - Energy	2	"Runes aglow, wisdom's seeds sow."
Copper Dragon - Copper	24	"Eyes of the soul, make us whole."
Crystal Dragon - Crystal	19	"Dreams take flight, in the runes' light."
Diamond Dragon - Diamond	25	"From earth to sky, blessings amplify."
Earth Dragon - Earth	6	"Blessings untold, ancient secrets unfold."
East Dragon - East	9	"Infinite skies, awaken wise."
Fire Dragon - Fire	5	"Dragon's breath, conquer life's depth."
Gold Dragon - Gold	22	"Earth's heartbeat, in these runes, repeat."
Ice Dragon - Ice	20	"Earth's embrace, in sacred space."
Iron Dragon - Iron	16	"Dragon's gaze, light up our ways."
Lava Dragon - Lava	21	"Earth's embrace, wisdom interlace."
Meteorite Dragon - Meteor	26	"From Earth's core, blessings pour."
Mind Dragon - Mind	12	"Ancient flame, bless every name."
North Dragon - North	8	"Harmony's song, in runes belong."
Rainbow Dragon - Light	1	"Dragons' embrace, bestow your grace."
Silver Dragon - Silver	23	"Eternal flame, bless each name."
Soul Dragon - Soul	13	"Ancient whispers, dreams take flight."
South Dragon - South	10	"Rune's allure, blessings pure."
Spirit Dragon - Spirit	7	"Guidance clear, in every sphere."
Stone Dragon - Stone	18	"Dragon's might, guide through the night."
Water Dragon - Life	3	"Rune and flame, your magic reclaim."
West Dragon - West	11	"Runes entwine, magic align."
Wood Dragon - Wood	17	"Dragon's lore, forever explore."

Dragon Runes Altar

You might like to create an Altar to use with your Dragon Runes, to assist in calling in and remembering the Dragons of the Runes. Here are examples of the Altars I set up, with the Rainbow Runes and the Wooden Runes.

This is my altar, The Dragon Runes are on a Dragon Shield (Viking), and in the centre is the Dragon Soul Tree called 'Dragon Heart', then the Chakra crystals covering the rainbow colours, a Dragon egg, numerous crystals, some representing my main Dragon guides, shells, wood, stones, hearts, feathers, and Lion headed bracelet :)

Wooden Altar:

Rainbow Altar:

Runes of Dragons

HALL OF DRAGON RUNES CEREMONY

If you prefer a guided Shamanic journey to the Dragons of the Runes, you can play the session I recorded and placed on YouTube, see { https://bit.ly/DragonRunes } and journey to the Hall of the Dragons of the Runes. This example is a journey to the Rainbow Dragon, you can use it to meet any Dragon of the Runes.

The following is that journey, you can follow in words if you prefer, rather than the video.

We Journey today with our Free Soul to Dartmoor and the Axis Mundi, which is our Portal to the Dragon Realm, which is down a Stone Staircase that I will open and hold, so we can move from this reality to the other world where it's easier for our spirit and our Dragons to meet.

This is a safe and secure world, where you can fly and walk on water and even breathe underwater. Time and space do not exist in the same manner, so you might feel like you went a very long way for a long time, and, in our time reality, it will be just 20 minutes.

FIRST and importantly centre yourself in the HEART, your spiritual heart just behind your Physical heart. Breath into that place and ask the mind to be still for the next while, as we adventure with the Dragons.

WE START in Dartmoor, in Devon.

Imagine for me a Bright Sunny day in England, all around for miles you see a vast expanse of vibrant green, your nose senses the smell of pine from the forests nearby and you see sheep and cows roaming free across the moorlands, munching on the lush green grass.

Overhead you hear the calls of the crows, the seagulls that have sheltered here overnight from the nearby coast. You see a hawk floating on the air currents above looking for its next meal and you spy the white tail of a rabbit as it darts between its burrows outsmarting the hawk above.

We walk through a wooden gateway, careful to close the gate and relatch the gate, so the sheep and cows and nearby Dartmoor ponies, do not leave the Dartmoor park, where its safe for them to wander freely.

A gravel path leads gently uphill, and we walk that, to our right we see the sparkling waters of the Fernworthy reservoir, we walk up hills past the ancient Oaks standing guard on the path.

The path meets a Y junction, and we walk upwards through the pine forest, keen noses will smell the pine, keen eyes will see the ponies and deer in the forest and your magic vision will see fairies and other beings in the woodlands

We walk further uphill and see a clearing in the forest and spy the stone circle in the middle. With reverence, we walk through the two stones that lead us down a short grassy path to the ancient and magical stone circle of Fernworthy.

We walk clockwise around the stone circle and find a stone that calls us, we sit by it or lean against it grounding ourselves with its solidity.

I'll open the portal

Once open I'll start drumming and you can with intention in mind "**Meet The Dragons of the Runes**" journey with me, down the stone stairs.

Let us walk down the stone stairs to the lower realm now as a group. We reach the bottom of the stairs, it's dark so I enlighten the staff in my hand, the CAVE is now bright and the floor surface is smooth from many feet over the centuries.

Follow me now through the CAVE, I knock on the dark wall of the CAVE to the Right and speak the magic words.

"Open Great Hall of the Dragon Runes"

A large ornate, covered in Dragon Runes, OAK door appears in the stone wall. Using the Dragon Door handle I pull the door open into the CAVE and one by one we walk through the door. It gently closes itself behind us.

We are standing in a corridor, it feels cool and it's bright, from some magical light source, so I close the light from my staff. The walls and ceiling of the corridor are covered in Dragon Runes, whilst the floor is smooth and even.

Ahead some 100 feet away there is natural sunlight and a shimmer of light plays across a stone circle. We walk towards the light and emerge into a glen, surrounded by mighty OAK trees.

As we appear at the entrance to the Glen, a large STONE OGRE walks out of the STONE WALL, one to the left and another to the RIGHT. They bid us welcome, and we offer them some of our food and supplies and any gifts we feel called to present, if you have none, bring something next time, as you will revisit here often on the Dragon Runes quest.

The STONE OGRES move off into the OAK Forest and enjoy the supplies we gifted them.

RUNES OF DRAGONS.

The Glen is circular, and vast, in its centre is a stone circle split into 28 sections, and on each of the sections is engraved into the creamy-brown stone a Rune of the Dragons, starting in the East is the first Rune, moving clockwise each rune, in turn, is shown, until we meet the WEST and here is an empty Rune stone, it has a slight dip in the middle, worn smooth by any feet over its existence.

You feel this is where you need to stand.

As you step onto the stone your world becomes etheric and wispy, and somehow you and everyone who entered the room is standing on the same stone all at once and yet in your own space! the paradox confuses your mind a little and opens your Spiritual heart deeply.

You breathe deeply and slowly to overcome any feelings of discomfort this space might bring to your body, and you relax.

SHAMANIC CALLING of the DRAGONS of the RUNES.

Ideally, PLAY a DRUM gently or play some drumming music.

"I ASK THE DRAGONS OF THE RUNES to JOIN us here NOW, we ASK for their WISDOM and INSIGHTS."

In your MIND ask for the DRAGONS OF THE RUNES TO APPEAR one by one at the STONE showing their RUNE.

Keep the DRUM playing while the DRAGONS JOIN us …..

You may see, or you may feel or sense or even smell the DRAGONS as they arrive in this SACRED Space.

"I BESEECH THE DRAGONS OF THE RUNES to JOIN us NOW to be introduced to the DRAGON RIDERS."

DRUM until all arrive or as many as can arrive of the twenty-seven Dragons….

"THANK YOU, GREAT DRAGON MASTERS, we ask for your blessings and wisdom, from here on we are in your SERVICE, please ask us what we may do for you, and we ask that you please answer our questions when we attend in the coming days and months and years."

"We call you ALL today to be introduced and we ask that when we CALL in the future you come and assist us, and we will assist you in any way we can."

"Please **SHARE** with us **EACH** any insights you feel would assist us in this quest to understand the Dragon Runes."

DRUM for a while, until you have heard from the Dragons.

"**Thank you, GREAT DRAGONS, we leave you now and thank you for your time and we will see you again soon.**"

WALK OUT

Once out and up the steps, stop the drumming.

Stand in the stone circle for a moment and then retrace your steps back down the hill, past the pine forest, right at the Y Junction and past the wise old Oaks, through the wooden gate and back into your body, stretch the toes, feet, calves, knees, thighs, toes, arms, hands, next, face and open the eyes and be fully back in your body, feeling refreshed.

You can repeat this journey every time you wish to call in one of the Dragons of the Runes, for example, call in the Soul Dragon and ask them for wisdom and insights. It will also in the beginning, assist, if you use the exercise suggested for each Dragon, it will help you to create a strong connection with the Dragon, and over time you will be able to journey to each Dragon with case and speed.

#1 The Meaning of the Rainbow Dragon

The mystical meaning of the Dragon rune for a Rainbow Dragon is a representation of hope and new beginnings.

This rune symbolises the potential for transformation and growth that lies within every individual.

It represents the power of the imagination and its ability to create new possibilities and opportunities.

It also speaks to the idea of embracing the unknown and embracing change.

The Rainbow Dragon's colours of the rainbow signify the seven chakras and the power of the creative life force.

This rune encourages the individual to look beyond their current circumstances and to recognise their inner strength and potential for growth.

It is a reminder that no matter how dark the world may seem, there is always the potential for growth and hope.

To tap into the full wisdom of the rune, go on a journey to the Hall and Glen of the Dragons of the Runes, and call in your Dragon, ask them questions you need answers to and, review the Rune and Artwork to help you connect fully to the Dragon of the Rune, and receive its wisdom and insight.

Runes of Dragons

The Rainbow Dragon Rune:

The Rainbow Dragon Art:

#2 The Meaning of the Chakra Dragon

The mystical meaning of the rune of the Chakra Dragon is a representation of the energy of the Dragon and its connection to the seven chakras of the body.

The rune can be used as a tool to help unlock and balance the power of the Dragon within, connecting it to the chakras and allowing for a deeper understanding of its power, the rune represents the energy of the Dragon and its connection to each of the seven chakras. The rune symbolises the Dragon's strength, courage, and wisdom, as well as its ability to heal, protect, and guide.

The rune can be used in meditation, visualisation, and other spiritual practices to help you align with and access the power of the Dragon within. The Dragon within is coiled around your spine, from Root Chakra to Crown, and tapping into that energy is what this rune is suggesting you do.

Runes of Dragons

The Chakra Dragon Rune:

The Chakra Dragon Art:

Exercise:

A great practice to use with this rune is a Chakra cleanse:

1. Lie down, close your eyes, get yourself comfortable, and ensure you are warm/cool enough:
2. Holding the rune in your hand place the hand with the rune over each Chakra (left or right hand - whichever feels right to you)
3. Place your NON-RUNE hand on your HEAD - CROWN Chakra [VIOLET] and it remains here for the 7 Chakras cleanse
4. Hold the RUNE Hand over your CROWN Chakra to cleanse, align, and imagine your Chakra Dragon sending healing energy to your CROWN Chakra [VIOLET]
5. Imagine each Chakra as a flower head, like a sunflower, full of petals, and see in your mind eye it rotating, either clockwise or anti-clockwise, and imagine each chakra eventually spinning together in unison, imagine dead petals being removed and replaced with vibrant new ones - thus cleansing the Chakra fully.
6. Hold the RUNE Hand over your 3rd EYE Chakra, to cleanse, align and imagine your Chakra Dragon sending healing energy to your FOREHEAD- 3rd EYE Chakra [INDIGO]
7. Hold the RUNE Hand over your THROAT CHAKRA to cleanse, align and imagine your Chakra Dragon sending healing energy to your THROAT- THROAT CHAKRA [BLUE]
8. Hold the RUNE Hand over your HEART CHAKRA to cleanse, align and imagine your Chakra Dragon sending healing energy to your HEART- HEART CHAKRA [GREEN]

9. Hold the RUNE Hand over your SOLAR PLEXUS CHAKRA to cleanse, align and imagine your Chakra Dragon sending healing energy to your belly button – SOLAR PLEXUS CHAKRA [YELLOW]
10. Hold the RUNE Hand over your SACRAL CHAKRA to cleanse, align and imagine your Chakra Dragon sending healing energy to your hand over your Womb/Hara - SACRAL CHAKRA [ORANGE]
11. Hold the RUNE Hand over your ROOT CHAKRA to cleanse, align and imagine your Chakra Dragon sending healing energy to the bottom of your spine - ROOT CHAKRA [RED]
12. Move the RUNE hand up and down from ROOT to CROWN and CROWN to ROOT three times to send bright vibrant healing light to your Chakra's

#3 The Meaning of the Water Dragon

The rune for a Water Dragon has a deep and mysterious meaning. It symbolises the journey of transformation and the power of the subconscious mind.

This rune reflects the mysterious and unknown depths of the sea and the power of intuition.

It speaks of a need to explore and understand the depths of our inner depths and hidden truths. It speaks of the power of imagination and creativity and encourages us to bring forth our highest potential.

It also speaks of our connection to the natural world and the power of the elements. This rune represents the need for courage to explore the unknown and the potential to rise above our challenges.

Exercise:

A great exercise for calling in the full powers of your Water Dragon is to immerse yourself in Water. Either a nice soak in a warm bath or for the adventurous how about a Sea swim?

Standing under a waterfall, as I did in Peru, is super cleansing and connecting to the raw power of Water. A shower at home to connect deeply with your Water Dragon will also work.

Another great option, if you do not mind the dark, is an isolation tank with salt water, you can float in it, like you can the Dead Sea, and relax and call in your Water Dragon.

Runes of Dragons

The Water Dragon Rune:

The Water Dragon Art:

#4 The Meaning of the Air Dragon

The mystical meaning of the rune for an Air Dragon is that it symbolises the power of transformation. This rune is often seen as a sign of the power of the mind, particularly the power of creativity, imagination, and vision. It encourages us to think outside of the box and to be open to new possibilities and ideas.

The Air Dragon is a symbol of the power of intuition and the ability to expand our horizons and explore the unknown. In addition, it suggests that our actions and decisions can be guided by our intuition and inner wisdom.

This rune is an invitation to explore the world of the unknown and trust our instincts to lead us in the right direction.

Exercise:

As you can imagine being in the wind would be a great way to connect to your Air Dragon. I often, normally each Friday, walk up to the top of the Tors on Dartmoor, and it's often very windy and refreshing. You could stand in the wind and call on your Air Dragon and commune in the wind.

Another option requiring less effort is to sit and breathe consciously in and out, whatever feels right at the time, and call in the Air Dragon with your breathing. I daily use the Wim Hod method for 2-3 rounds of breathing.

The two sample breathwork exercises at the start of the course - Box breath and Dragon breath would be useful to use here too. Another option requiring less effort is to sit and breathe consciously in and out, whatever feels right at the time, and call in the Air Dragon with your breathing.

Runes of Dragons

The Air Dragon Rune:

The Air Dragon Art:

#5 The Meaning of the Fire Dragon

The rune for a Fire Dragon has a deep, mystical meaning. It is a rune of strength, passion, and creativity.

It is an emblem of courage and boldness and a symbol of transformation and renewal.

It is also a reminder of the power of the imagination and the importance of trust in your abilities.

It is a reminder to stay true to our vision and never give up in the face of adversity.

The Fire Dragon is a sign of our ability to create and manifest our dreams, even when it may seem impossible.

The rune is a reminder that we can always harness the power of our passions and our strength to make a difference in the world.

Exercise:

A great way to connect with your Fire Dragon is through Fire :)

Sit by the roaring fire and call in your Fire Dragon, and do NOT be surprised if you see them in the Flames, dancing away, I see them each time.

If you cannot have a roaring fire, then light a candle or a match! and have the ceremony of connecting like that.

Runes of Dragons

The Fire Dragon Rune:

The Fire Dragon Art:

#6 The Meaning of the Earth Dragon

The rune for an Earth Dragon is the symbol of groundedness, stability, and security. Its energy is that of a foundation that is unshakeable and connected to the Earth.

It symbolises the power of the Earth Dragon to manifest and create that which it desires. It is a reminder that one must be rooted in the present and be open to the potential of the future.

This rune is also a symbol of personal growth, as it is believed that the Earth Dragon will help its owner to grow, learn, and evolve. It is a reminder to stay connected to the Earth and to embrace the power of the present.

The Earth Dragon is a reminder that we are all connected to the same source of energy and that we can create our destiny.

Exercise:

This one is the simplest I think, take your shoes and socks off and stand with bare feet on the Earth.

Try this on the true Earth, not flooring or concrete, stand in the Sand, On the Grass, in the Mud.

And connect to the Earth below your feet, imagine a root growing from the heel of each foot into the ground, connecting you to the Earth.

If you cannot stand on the bare Earth, then standing in your house or apartment will suffice, just imagine your roots running down through the carpet, flooring, and into the Earth below.

Call on your Earth Dragon to connect with you.

The Earth Dragon Rune:

The Earth Dragon Art:

#7 The Meaning of the Spirit Dragon

This Spirit Dragon rune holds a mystical meaning as the Wheel of Fortune.

This rune represents the cycle of life and the constant change and transformation that comes with it.

For a Spirit Dragon, this rune signifies the need for balance and embracing the ups and downs of life. It reminds us that all things come and go in their own time and to trust the process.

To not hold onto this as being permanent and to know that all things are transient. The Wheel of Fortune also speaks to the power of destiny and the Dragon's role in shaping your fate.

Ask your Spirit Dragon how they can assist you.

Exercise:

You might hope that drinking spirit might connect to your Spirit Dragon!

You can connect deeper to your Spirit Dragon by connecting to yourself and your Soul essence, you are a Soul with a Body, so connect to the Soul that has this body, feel your Soul and your spirit essence, and use that to call on your Spirit Dragon.

Runes of Dragons

The Spirit Dragon Rune:

The Spirit Dragon Art:

#8 The Meaning of the North Dragon

The rune of the North Dragon holds the mystical meaning of The High Priestess. This rune represents intuition, reflection, and knowledge.

It invites you to trust the inner voice and use your inner knowledge to guide you on your spiritual journey.

The rune also urges you through the North Dragon to seek a balance between your inner and outer worlds to manifest your desires and fulfill your purpose.

The High Priestess guides you to trust the unknown and your intuition, encouraging you to embrace the mysteries of life.

A Dragon high priestess combines the power and mysticism of Dragons with the wisdom and spirituality of a high priestess. Often portrayed as a powerful and wise leader who is respected and revered by both dragons and humans alike.

Exercise:

Do you know where the true North Point is?

If not find a compass and stand with your body facing North and call on the direction North to assist you in connecting to your North Dragon and call upon your high priestess energy, found in your inner feminine, whether you have a male or female essence.

Runes of Dragons

The North Dragon Rune:

The North Dragon Art:

#9 The Meaning of the East Dragon

The rune for an East Dragon holds a mystical meaning of resilience and strength.

It signifies that the holder has overcome challenges and obstacles in their life and has emerged stronger and more determined.

The rune also represents the need to defend oneself from future challenges, and to do so with a sense of optimism and faith.

The East Dragon encourages you to continue to stand firm in your own beliefs and values and be ready to navigate new and exciting opportunities in the journey ahead.

Exercise:

Do you know the truth East direction?

If not find a compass and stand facing your body to the East and ask the Direction of the East to assist you in calling upon your East Dragon.

The sun rises in the East, if you can sit and watch the sunrise that would be a powerful way to connect with the East Dragon.

Runes of Dragons

The East Dragon Rune:

The East Dragon Art:

#10 The Meaning of the South Dragon

The rune that represents a South Dragon holds mystical significance as it embodies the energy of the spiritual fire, an inner fire, which is associated with inspiration, passion, and transformation.

This rune symbolises creativity, ambition, and a desire to succeed.

The holder of the South Dragon rune is encouraged to embrace their inner fire, to be spontaneous, and to trust their instincts.

It also carries a warning to not be consumed by your flames, to maintain control, and to channel their energy into positive endeavours.

Ultimately, this rune calls for the holder of the South Dragon rune to harness their inner fire and use it to fuel their journey toward success and enlightenment.

Exercise:

Do you know the truth South direction?

If not find a compass and stand facing your body to the South and ask the Direction of the South to assist you in calling upon your South Dragon.

Runes of Dragons

The South Dragon Rune:

The South Dragon ART:

#11 The Meaning of the West Dragon

The West Dragon rune represents intuition, deep knowledge, inner wisdom, and the presence of a spiritual guide that is leading them toward enlightenment.

The rune urges you to trust your insight and inner voice in making decisions.

This rune also suggests that secrets and hidden knowledge may be revealed to you via the West Dragon, which will further aid you in the journey toward self-discovery.

Overall, this rune serves as a reminder from the West Dragon to listen to your inner wisdom and trust in the unknown journey ahead.

Exercise:

Do you know the truth West direction?

If not find a compass and stand facing your body to the West and ask the Direction of the West to assist you in calling upon your West Dragon.

The Sun sets in the West, a great way to connect to your West Dragon would be to sit and watch the sun setting.

Runes of Dragons

The West Dragon Rune:

The West Dragon Art:

#12 The Meaning of the Mind Dragon

The Mind Dragon rune symbolises strength, power, and good fortune.

It also represents the inner fire and passion within oneself that needs to be unleashed or controlled.

This rune may signify that change is imminent, and that one must tap into their inner reserves to overcome any obstacles.

Overall, the Mind Dragon rune represents transformation, courage, and a bold spirit.

Exercise:

The mind is a busy thing, always working with many thoughts, often scattered, we do not want to be in this mind state when connecting to the Dragons.

I always say turn off the mind and come into the Heart and that is what we need to do here too.

Relax yourself physically, take some relaxing breaths, and sit or lie down, closing the eyes is Key, as it turns the mind processing & thinking about what you are seeing, and the brain can relax, and once it does, go into the Heart-Mind.

You know it, place your essence in the Heart and use the Mind of the Heart to call your Mind Dragon in.

The Mind Dragon Rune:

The Mind Dragon Art:

#13 The Meaning of the Soul Dragon

The Soul Dragon rune represents the spirit and inner strength that lies within us all, the interpretation centres around wisdom, intuition, and inner transformation.

The rune symbolises a need for deep reflection and self-discovery during these times of change.

To look within oneself and review all that one thinks one knows and see if it's a truth that still resonates at a soul level.

It's a strong push to have you review who you are and what your soul's mission is on Earth at this tumultuous time.

Exercise:

Relax by sitting or lying down and fully relax the body, close your eyes, and chill out fully.

You are NOT your body; you are the Soul, and you have a body.

From this perspective call in the Soul Dragon.

Runes of Dragons

The Soul Dragon Rune:

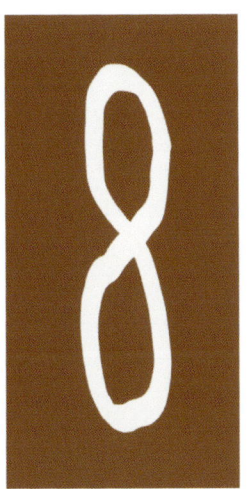

The Soul Dragon Art:

#14 The Meaning of the Body Dragon

The Body Dragon rune represents a unique and mystical symbolism that combines elements of strength, power, and transformation.

The Body Dragon rune depicts a Person and Dragon with a robust and *muscular physique, representing physical strength and vitality, a formidable force, mirroring the indomitable spirit within.

*This may be more of a depiction of your truest body image rather than your physical one, your spiritual body will be the finest version of your physical essence.

It embodies the idea that we possess immense power within ourselves, which, when harnessed properly, can manifest great change and resilience.

This rune urges us to embrace change, to let go of outdated patterns and beliefs, and to embrace personal growth.

It emphasises that transformation and evolution are not only possible but necessary for progress.

Exercise:

Hug yourself, caress your whole body, and thank it for hosting your Soul.

Truly feel into the physical body and from this perspective call on your Body Dragon.

The Body Dragon Rune:

The Body Dragon Art:

#15 The Meaning of the Aura Dragon

The Aura Dragon symbolises the convergence of ancient wisdom, spirituality, and personal transformation.

This rune is characterised by its art's vibrant colours, intricate patterns, and ethereal energy, reflecting the profound connection to the spiritual realm that the Aura Dragon embodies.

As a creature of immense power and grace, the Aura Dragon represents the awakening of one's inner magic and connection to the divine.

When this rune appears, it signifies that profound spiritual growth and enlightenment are on the horizon. The Aura Dragon is often associated with the concept of aura, which refers to the subtle energy field that surrounds and interpenetrates all living beings.

This rune encourages us to tap into our own aura, to explore the depths of our own energy and gain a deeper understanding of our true selves. Additionally, the Aura Dragon represents the merging of the physical and spiritual realms, reminding us that we are not separate from the cosmic energies that surround us and rather an integral part of the fabric of the universe.

Exercise:

Like the Chakra Dragon rune, the Aura Dragon rune works best when you go through an Aura Cleanse with the intention of connecting to the Aura Dragon.

You can do that on this webinar I ran, see https://bit.ly/EnglishMysticAura

The Aura Dragon Rune:

The Aura Dragon Art:

#16 The Meaning of the Iron Dragon

The Iron Dragon symbolises strength, power, and resilience, this rune brings forth a unique blend of energies that intertwine both the earthly and the fantastical aspects of life.

In its essence, the Iron Dragon signifies the embodiment of unwavering determination and unyielding will.

Just as the Dragon's scales are impenetrable and unbreakable, this rune suggests that one possesses an inner strength that cannot be easily diminished.

It urges the querent to tap into their reservoirs of resilience, pushing forward against challenges and obstacles in their path.

Moreover, the Iron Dragon embodies the power to overcome and conquer adversity.

It serves as a reminder that, while life may present formidable trials and tribulations, one can rise above them.

Exercise:

To assist in calling on your Iron Dragon find a piece of iron you can hold while calling the Dragon in.

It can be a small piece of iron or a larger one, common items made from iron in the house are:

Nails, Saws, Hammers, Drills, Hinges, Door handles, Window latches, Fireplace grills, and Stoves.

Runes of Dragons

The Iron Dragon Rune:

The Iron Dagon Art:

#17 The Meaning of the Wood Dragon

The Wood Dragon is a fascinating creature deeply woven into the mystical realm and represents an intricate blend of natural elements, intuition, growth, and transformation. With its association to the element of Wood, it signifies the power of growth and expansion.

It embodies the energy of blooming potential and the ability to adapt skillfully to changing circumstances. It symbolises the resilience and vitality found in the heart of nature itself.

The holder of this rune can take on the power of vitality, strength, and raw power of the Dragons and be harmonious and nurturing, the Wood Dragon guides and supports your personal growth. The Wood Dragon embodies these characteristics to provide profound insights and guidance to seekers. It represents a period of profound transformation and personal growth.

The rune suggests that the holder is entering a phase of transition, where they have the potential to harness the power of their intuition and tap into their deepest desires, for the mystical, transformation, balance, and unity. It invites individuals to embrace their innate power of intuition and adaptability and to journey through life with grace and wisdom.

Exercise:

A great exercise to call on your Wood Dragon is to hug a Tree! If you do not have access to a tree, then a piece of wood, even a wooden spoon will assist you in creating a strong connection with your Wood Dragon. Wooden flooring will assist too.

Runes of Dragons

The Wood Dragon Rune:

The Wood Dragon Art:

#18 The Meaning of the Stone Dragon

The Stone Dragon carries profound mystical meanings that symbolise strength, stability, and resilience.

This rune represents the majestic power, wisdom, and grounded energy of the stone dragon.

As we delve into its mystical interpretation, we are invited to explore the following symbolism:

Stone symbolism

A. Strength and Endurance: The Stone Dragon embodies unwavering strength and endurance. It signifies an unwavering force that is unyielding in the face of challenges. Just as a stone dragon remains solid and unaffected by external influences, this rune suggests embracing inner strength to overcome obstacles.

B. Grounding Energy: The Stone Dragon is deeply connected to the earth element, representing grounding and stability. It serves as a reminder to anchor oneself in the present moment, cultivating a sense of stability and resilience within our lives. The rune suggests finding balance and remaining steadfast during chaos or upheaval.

C. Wisdom and Patience: The Stone Dragon rune is associated with ancient wisdom and patience. It represents a calm and composed energy that invites us to contemplate our actions and decisions with wisdom. This rune encourages us to approach situations with a measured perspective and to trust that time will reveal the answers we seek.

Runes of Dragons

The Stone Dragon Rune:

The Stone Dragon Art:

Stone symbolism continued..

D. Protection and Guardianship: The Stone Dragon is a powerful protector and guardian. It acts as a shield against negative energies, safeguarding against potential harm. This rune reminds us to draw strength from our inner guardian, encouraging us to establish healthy boundaries and protect our well-being.

E. Resilience and Transformation: The stone dragon, being a creature of durable stone material, embodies resilience and transformation. It suggests that even in the face of adversity, we can adapt and grow. This rune encourages us to embrace change, viewing obstacles as opportunities for personal transformation and evolution.

In summary, the mystical meaning of the rune for a Stone Dragon encompasses strength, stability, wisdom, protection, and resilience. This rune serves as a powerful metaphor, inviting us to tap into our inner power, reconnect with the earth's grounding energy, and embrace the transformative journey that lies ahead.

Exercise:

Grab a stone, small or large, and hold it in your hands, or sit on a large rock out in nature and connect to the Stone to help you call upon your Stone Dragon.

Runes of Dragons

#19 The Meaning of the Crystal Dragon

The Crystal Dragon is a powerful and enigmatic creature that embodies both the awe-inspiring beauty of crystals and the majestic strength of Dragons.

When associated with a rune, the mystical meaning takes on a unique significance, symbolising a potent blend of wisdom, abundance, and profound transformation. Crystal Dragon represents the fusion of the crystal's healing energy and the Dragon's metaphysical fire.

It is a rune that embodies the union of spiritual illumination and personal power, offering valuable insights and opportunities for growth. At its core, the Crystal Dragon signifies clarity of perception and a deep connection to one's intuition.

The Dragon's wisdom, as represented in this context, allows individuals to see through illusions and uncover the truth within themselves and their surroundings. It encourages individuals to trust their instincts and tap into their inner knowledge when confronting challenges or making important decisions. Crystals are known for their vibrational energies and their ability to harness the Earth's natural forces.

Exercise:

Grab a Crystal or three, If you do not yet own a Crystal! what have you been up to :). I suggest strongly going to a crystal shop and finding one that calls you! yes, they do that and so will many others, they are very addictive :)

Hold a favourite crystal or more in hand or hands and call upon the Crystals to assist you in connecting with your Crystal Dragon.

The Crystal Dragon Rune:

The Crystal Dragon Art:

#20 The Meaning of the Ice Dragon

An Ice Dragon holds a profound mystical meaning that encompasses the essence and symbolism of this majestic creature.

Representing power, mystery, and the element of ice, this rune offers insights into the qualities and energies embodied by the ice dragon.

At its core, the ice dragon rune symbolises strength and resilience.

Just as ice can withstand the harshest winters, the ice dragon signifies the ability to overcome challenges and endure difficult situations with grace. This rune suggests that one possesses an indomitable spirit and that one should draw upon their inner power and determination when faced with adversity.

Furthermore, the Ice Dragon rune embodies the concept of duality. On one hand, the Ice Dragon epitomises coldness and detachment, suggesting the need for emotional distance and objectivity.

This rune advises maintaining a level-headed approach and avoiding becoming too emotionally swayed by external influences. On the other hand, the Ice Dragon also signifies the potential for transformation and growth, as ice can melt and give life to new beginnings.

Runes of Dragons

The Ice Dragon Rune:

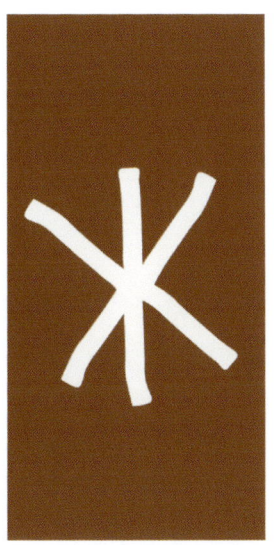

The Ice Dragon Art:

It encourages individuals to tap into their emotions and explore their depths, reminding them that vulnerability and change can lead to personal evolution.

In the mystical realm, the Ice Dragon rune also represents mystery and hidden knowledge.

The secretive nature of the Ice Dragon invites individuals to embrace their intuitive abilities and explore the depths of their subconscious.

It is a reminder to trust one's instincts and delve into the unknown with an open mind, as there may be valuable insights and wisdom waiting to be discovered.

Ultimately, the rune for an Ice Dragon holds a mystical meaning that incorporates resilience, duality, transformation, and hidden knowledge. It serves as a reminder to embrace one's inner strength, maintain emotional balance, be open to change, and trust intuitive guidance.

By embodying these qualities, one can harness the power of the ice dragon and navigate life's challenges with grace and confidence.

Exercise:

You have two options here, grab an ice cube (lolly, ice cream) and hold, ingest, and use the ice-cold to help you connect with your Ice Dragon, or find yourself an ICE Bath and sit in it while you connect to your Ice Dragon, Yes, I've done that with the Wim Hof group locally, it's VERY Refreshing :)!

Runes of Dragons

#21 The Meaning of the Lava Dragon

The Lava Dragon holds deep mystical significance.

As a creature of both raw power and fiery energy, the Lava Dragon embodies a range of symbolic meanings that resonate with the human psyche.

Firstly, the Lava Dragon rune represents transformation and intense change.

Just as molten lava reshapes the terrain it passes through, this rune suggests that major transformations are coming your way.

It indicates a period of upheaval and self-discovery, urging you to embrace change and channel your inner resilience.

Furthermore, the lava dragon rune symbolises passion and desire. The Dragon's fiery nature is often associated with intense emotions, representing a surge of burning energy that fuels your ambitions and desires.

It encourages you to tap into your inner passions and pursue them with fervour and determination. Additionally, this rune conveys strength and courage.

Runes of Dragons

The Lava Dragon Rune:

The Lava Dragon Art:

The Lava Dragon's formidable presence demonstrates the need to harness your inner strength and face challenges head-on. It serves as a reminder that you possess the power and resilience to overcome obstacles and achieve your goals. Embrace your inner fire and allow it to guide you on your journey.

Moreover, the Lava Dragon rune signifies the sacred union of opposites. Its fiery nature intertwines with the symbolic element of earth, representing the union of passion and stability, of action and grounding. It offers a reminder that finding a balance between opposing forces is essential in maintaining harmony in your life.

Lastly, the Lava Dragon signifies untapped potential and hidden powers. You are being urged to explore hidden talents and abilities within yourself. Unlocking your true potential can lead to great accomplishments and personal growth.

In summary, the rune representing a Lava Dragon holds mystical meaning rooted in transformation, passion, strength, balance, and untapped potential. It serves as a powerful reminder for you to embrace change, channel your passion, tap into your inner strength, seek balance, and harness your hidden powers to achieve personal evolution and accomplish your deepest desires.

Exercise:

There are always options and the safest is to buy a piece of Lava, it will be cool and easy to hold :) or grab your big pants and go on an adventure to a volcano and feel the heat, smell the air, feel the ground shake, and try to connect deeply to your Lava Dragon. I'm still to do the volcano visit :)

Runes of Dragons

#22 The Meaning of the Gold Dragon

A Gold Dragon holds profound mystical significance, reflecting the majestic and mysterious aspects associated with these mythical creatures.

Gold dragons are revered as benevolent beings embodying wisdom, power, and enlightenment.

The Gold Dragon rune symbolises abundance, transformation, and spiritual ascension.

At its core, the Gold Dragon rune represents the awakening of ancient wisdom within oneself.

It signifies a deep connection to the higher realms, urging individuals to embrace spiritual growth and explore their full potential.

The appearance of this rune suggests that the seeker may be at the threshold of a profound internal transformation, evolving into a wiser and more enlightened version of themselves.

The Gold Dragon is intimately connected to the element of fire, which ignites passion, ambition, and creativity.

When this rune appears, it signifies the manifestation of one's highest ambitions and goals. Just as the gold dragon breathes fire, it imparts the strength and determination needed to overcome obstacles and achieve success. This rune encourages individuals to harness their inner power and use it wisely to manifest abundance and achieve a sense of fulfillment in life.

Runes of Dragons

The Gold Dragon Rune:

The Gold Dragon Art:

Moreover, the Gold Dragon also carries a message of protection and guidance. Just as dragons are revered as guardians, this card serves as a reminder that spiritual guardianship is present in the seeker's life. It signifies that divine forces are supporting their journey, offering guidance and protection along the way.

In terms of relationships and emotions, the appearance of the Gold Dragon rune suggests a deep sense of self-assurance and inner strength. It signifies a period of growth and transformation within relationships, allowing for the dissolution of old patterns and the emergence of a more harmonious and fulfilling connection.

This rune encourages individuals to embrace their authenticity and communicate their needs from a place of empowerment and self-love.

In summary, the mystical meaning of the Gold Dragon rune encompasses the themes of abundance, transformation, spiritual awakening, and protection. Its presence indicates a powerful and transformative period in the seeker's life, urging them to embrace their inner wisdom, tap into their unlimited potential, and manifest their desires.

Exercise:

Hold a Gold object, a wedding ring for example on/in your hand, if you do not have real Gold use something that looks Gold in colour, may coins do, and use that to assist you in connecting with your Gold Dragon.

Runes of Dragons

#23 The Meaning of the Silver Dragon

The Silver Dragon is a majestic and powerful creature that holds significant mystical symbolism in the realm of runes.

Representing wisdom, intuition, and transformation, the rune associated with the silver dragon embodies both the ethereal and earthly planes, offering profound spiritual insights and guidance.

The appearance of a Silver Dragon signifies the presence of ancient knowledge and higher consciousness. The Dragon's silver scales glisten with the essence of enlightenment, reflecting its deep connection to the spiritual realms.

It serves as a reminder to tap into one's inner wisdom and intuition, encouraging individuals to trust their instincts and seek truth within themselves. Inherently magical by nature, the silver dragon embodies a powerful transformational energy.

Just as the dragon goes through cycles of growth and change in its lifetime, this rune indicates the need for individuals to embrace transformation and growth. It suggests that embracing change will bring forth new opportunities, allowing individuals to soar to unimaginable heights on their spiritual journey. Moreover, the silver dragon represents a harmonious balance between mystical realms and the physical world.

It symbolises the integration of spirituality and practicality, teaching individuals to unite their spiritual beliefs with their day-to-day lives.

Runes of Dragons

The Silver Dragon Rune:

The Silver Dragon Art:

The Silver Dragon reminds us to seek spiritual understanding while remaining grounded and connected to our physical reality.

It urges individuals to explore esoteric knowledge and expand their spiritual horizons. It signifies a time of heightened intuition and encourages individuals to delve deeper into their spiritual practices.

It also serves as a reminder to trust the guidance of the universe, for the silver dragon is a guiding force that offers protection and guidance along the spiritual path.

In conclusion, the rune depicting a silver dragon holds mystical significance, representing wisdom, intuition, transformation, and the harmonious balance between the spiritual and physical realms.

It encourages individuals to tap into their inner wisdom, embrace transformation, and seek spiritual understanding while remaining grounded in their daily lives.

The Silver Dragon rune serves as a symbol of guidance and protection on one's spiritual journey, opening doors to profound insights and spiritual growth.

Exercise:

Hold a silver object in your hand, a candle stick, ring, or an object that is silver in colour, and connect using that silver to your Silver Dragon.

Runes of Dragons

#24 The Meaning of the Copper Dragon

The Copper Dragon holds a profound mystical meaning that intertwines the symbolism of dragons and the essence of copper.

This rune unfolds a tale of intricate power, balance, transformation, and mysticism.

At its core, the Copper Dragon signifies the harmonious fusion of dualities. It embodies the spirit of balance, represented by the elemental forces of fire and earth.

The fiery nature of dragons aligns with transformative energies, while the stability and grounding energy of copper aligns with the suit of Pentacles. (Pentacles represent the element of Earth and the material world.)

The Pentacles symbolize earthly matters, such as finances, work, health, and the physical realm. They are associated with abundance, stability, and practicality. The imagery of the Pentacle often depicts wealth, resources, and material possessions.

When the Pentacle appears in a reading, it typically indicates matters related to money, career, or physical well-being. They can represent opportunities for growth, financial stability, or a focus on practical matters.

The Pentacle & Cooper Dragon rune can also indicate a need for grounding, a reminder to care for your physical body or the importance of creating a solid foundation in your endeavours.

The Copper Dragon Rune:

The Copper Dragon Art:

Overall, it highlights the practical aspects of life and emphasizes the importance of the physical realm, resources, and material well-being.

As a creature of magic, the Copper Dragon symbolises the liberation of the creative spirit. It encourages us to tap into our potential and rise above limitations, granting us the ability to manifest our desires and dreams. This rune serves as a catalyst for exploring hidden talents, acting as a guide in unleashing our inner power and embracing our unique abilities.

Copper, known for its conductivity, contributes to the rune's mystical meaning by symbolising deep connections with the intangible realms.

It invites us to embrace our intuitive wisdom and trust in our instincts. The presence of the Copper Dragon suggests that the answers we seek lie within us, waiting to be discovered if only we listen to our inner voice.

Furthermore, the Copper Dragon is a gatekeeper of the unknown, encouraging us to face our fears and explore uncharted territories with courage.

This mighty creature grants protection and acts as a guardian against malevolent forces, inspiring strength, and resilience.

Its appearance as a rune signals the need to confront challenges head-on and embark on a transformative journey toward personal growth.

In its majestic presence, the Copper Dragon offers transcendence and spiritual evolution.

It carries the wisdom of ancient realms and invites us to expand our consciousness, reconnecting with the mystical forces that are hidden in plain sight.

This rune serves as a reminder that there is always more to explore and comprehend in the realms of magic, awakening our desire for spiritual exploration and enlightening our path.

In conclusion, the mystical meaning of the rune for a Copper Dragon combines the powerful symbolism of dragons with the transformative properties of copper. It represents balance, creative expression, psychic intuition, protection, and spiritual growth.

By embodying the spirit of the Copper Dragon, we are urged to embark on a mystical journey of self-discovery and embrace the magic that lies within and around us.

Exercise:

Hold something made of Copper, a pot, a piece of copper pipe, or something copper in colour in your hand, and use that copper-ness to connect to your Copper Dragon.

#25 The Meaning of the Diamond Dragon

The Diamond Dragon is a captivating rune that holds deep mystical symbolism and carries profound meaning.

Representing strength, wisdom, and transformation, this rune holds a mystical connection to the spiritual realm and offers guidance in times of change and growth.

In its essence, the Diamond Dragon signifies strength and resilience. Just as a diamond is formed under immense pressure, the Dragon represents the ability to overcome adversity and emerge stronger and more brilliant.

It symbolises the power within us to navigate through life's challenges with grace and determination, reminding us to stay strong in the face of obstacles.

Wisdom is another significant aspect attributed to the Diamond Dragon. Much like our ancient and wise Dragons, this rune encourages us to tap into our inner wisdom and intuition. It reminds us to trust our instincts and seek clarity in our thoughts and actions

The Diamond Dragon reflects the importance of self-reflection and introspection to gain deeper insights into our lives and make informed decisions. At its core, the Diamond Dragon also represents transformation and change. Just as a diamond undergoes a metamorphosis from carbon to a beautiful gem, this rune heralds a period of personal growth and transformation in one's life. It signifies that a profound change is approaching and encourages embracing this change with courage and acceptance.

The Diamond Dragon Art:

The Diamond Dragon Art:

The Diamond Dragon reminds us that true transformation often requires stepping out of our comfort zones and embracing new possibilities. Furthermore, this rune holds an element of mystery and mysticism. The Diamond Dragon whispers secrets and hidden knowledge from the depths of the universe.

It invites us to explore the mysteries of life and engage in spiritual pursuits. Through meditation, contemplation, or connecting with spiritual guides, the Diamond Dragon encourages us to seek higher truths and connect with our spiritual selves.

In summary, the rune of the Diamond Dragon encompasses strength, wisdom, transformation, and mystery.

Its mystical meaning encourages the seeker to find inner strength, tap into their wisdom, embrace transformation, and explore the spiritual side of life. The rune serves as a reminder that, like the Dragon, we can navigate through life's challenges and emerge as resilient beings.

Exercise:

Hold a diamond in your hand, maybe you have one in a ring or earring? If you do not have access to a diamond, use something glass and sparkling to assist you in connecting to your Diamond Dragon.

Runes of Dragons

#26 The Meaning of the Meteorite Dragon

The Meteor Dragon is a symbol of profound transformation and celestial energy.

It represents the merging of earthly and cosmic forces, presenting a powerful and transformative journey.

The rune depicts a majestic Dragon soaring through a starry sky, leaving a trail of stardust in its wake.

This imagery symbolises the Dragon's connection to the celestial realm and its ability to harness the energy of the cosmos.

In its mystical meaning, the Meteor Dragon rune signifies a significant shift and change in one's life.

It suggests that unforeseen events or opportunities may come your way, altering the course of your journey.

Just as a meteor showers unexpected blessings upon the earth, this card conveys the idea of unexpected breakthroughs, revelations, and possibilities.

The Meteor Dragon prompts you to embrace change and to let go of old patterns and beliefs that no longer serve you. It encourages you to trust in the unknown and be open to the cosmic influences guiding you. This rune holds the potential for immense personal growth and expansion, as you harness the transformative energies of the universe.

Runes of Dragons

The Meteorite Dragon RUNE:

The Meteorite Dragon Art:

Additionally, the Meteor Dragon represents the power and magic that lies within you. It reminds you to tap into your inner strength, resilience, and adaptability. Like the dragon, you possess a fiery spirit and the ability to rise above challenges, no matter how daunting they may seem.

In readings, the appearance of the Meteor Dragon may suggest that a profound spiritual awakening is on the horizon.

It may imply the need to explore spiritual practices, seek guidance and wisdom from higher realms, or deepen your connection with the divine.

Ultimately, the mystical meaning of the Meteor Dragon is a call to embrace change, trust in the cosmic forces at play, and allow yourself to evolve and soar to new heights.

By embracing this rune's energy, you can embark on a transformative journey with newfound purpose, wisdom, and enlightenment.

Exercise:

You can purchase bits of a meteorite from online & local stores, purchase a small piece, or find yourself a meteorite locally!

I sat on one in Peru it was large and for sale for hundreds of thousands of dollars, it wouldn't fit in my suitcase, so it stayed in Peru!

Use the connection with the meteorite to connect with your Meteorite Dragon.

Runes of Dragons

#27 The Meaning of the Blank Dragon

The blank rune, also known as the Wyrm rune, holds an intriguing and mystical meaning in runic divination.

Unlike other runes, which have specific symbols and interpretations, the blank rune is a symbol of mystery and the unknown. One interpretation of the blank rune is that it represents a hidden potential or hidden knowledge.

It signifies the presence of unseen forces or energies that are at play in a situation. When drawn in a reading, the blank rune may suggest that there is more to a situation than meets the eye and urges the seeker to delve deeper into the mysteries surrounding it.

Another aspect of the blank rune is its association with the concept of chaos and unpredictability. It may indicate a period of uncertainty or instability in one's life. This rune reminds us that life is filled with constant change and that embracing this change, even if it seems frightening or uncomfortable, can lead to personal growth and transformation.

Furthermore, the blank rune carries a message of intuition and trusting one's instincts. It encourages the seeker to rely on their inner wisdom and instincts rather than seeking external guidance.

The Blank Rune:

The Blank Rune Art:

This rune invites exploration of the subconscious mind and awakening of intuition, offering insights and guidance from within. In essence, the blank rune symbolises the unlimited potential of the cosmos and the vastness of the human experience. It serves as a reminder that there is always more to learn, discover, and explore on our journey through life.

Drawing the blank rune in a reading calls for contemplation, reflection, and embracing the unknown with curiosity and an open mind.

Exercise:

That meditation thing where you empty your mind, no not that, to be truly Blank you need to be reset to your starting point, back to original source. That is possible in a POWERFUL Shamanic ceremony that you only need to do a few times unless you plan on being a Shaman.

It's a Dismemberment Journey where your Spirit Guides (for example your Dragons) remove your physicalness and return you to pure energy, before rebuilding you back!

Try it (https://bit.ly/dismembermentjourney) and then connect to the Blank rune and see what it has for you!

On mobile scan this QR code:

EnglishMystic

A seasoned entrepreneur, and Information Technology expert with nearly four decades in the field, now a master in the mystical realms.

Based near the enchanting Dartmoor National Park in Devon, England, I've delved deep into the world of energy healing within Shamanism, becoming a Reiki master, Rahanni celestial energy healer, and a dedicated practitioner of ancient Shamanic arts.

It doesn't stop there, my connection with Dragons is a central part of the journey.

I'm not only a Dragon Shaman but also a passionate teacher, spreading the wisdom of Shamanism and guiding people on how to connect with their very own spirit team and particularly Dragon guides.

Meet Your Dragon Guides:
https://www.meetyourdragons.com/

Web: https://www.englishmystic.com/

Facebook: https://www.facebook.com/EnglishMystic

Instagram: https://www.instagram.com/englishmystic/
YouTube:
https://www.youtube.com/@KevinHumphreyVideo

TikTok: https://www.tiktok.com/@englishmystic

Linkedin: https://www.linkedin.com/in/englishmystic/

Books by Kevin Humphrey / EnglishMystic

MERLIN, THE MYSTICAL BARD, Transmissions, Spells & Chants

Galactic Mysticism: EnglishMystic's, Ritual and Ceremony for Healing and Wisdom

Author of Fly With Dragons by Kevin Humphrey

All available on the Amazon website.

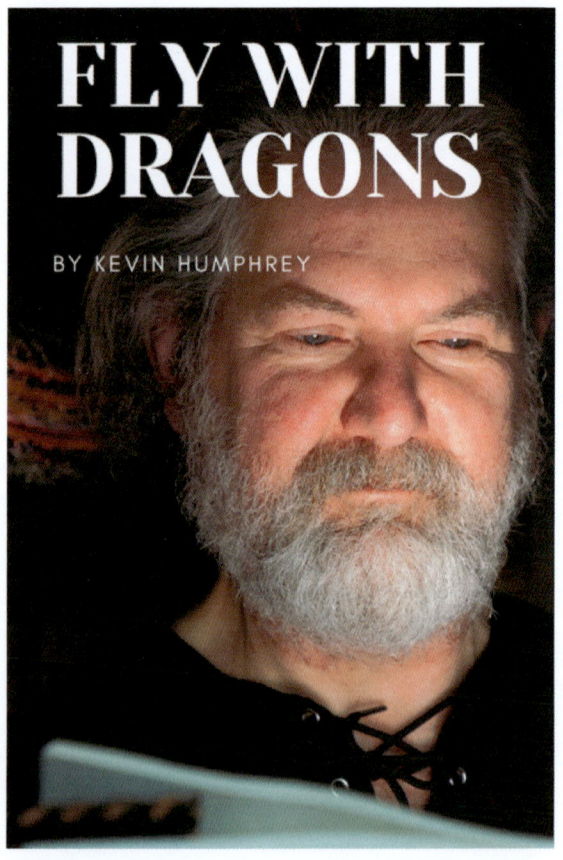

Links

If the bit.ly links do not work, you can use the originals as below:

https://bit.ly/DragonRunes is also https://youtu.be/c-PoPH4pWuw

https://bit.ly/dismembermentjourney is also https://www.englishmystic.com/blog/the-dismemberment-shamanic-journey-with-englishmystic

https://bit.ly/EnglishMysticAura is also https://www.englishmystic.com/blog/16th-may-2023-shamanism-heals-aura-cleanse

THE

END

IS

ANOTHER

BEGINNING ……..

Printed in Great Britain
by Amazon